ESCAPE

'It's a very beautiful day. Oh, I forget – you can't go out. Ha, ha, ha!' says the prison guard. Brown is in prison – for five years! All he can do is read. The prison guard hates him and gives him bad food. 'This is no life. I must get out of here,' he thinks.

Then one day, he looks out of his very small window and he sees a bird. 'That bird is free,' he thinks. Suddenly he has an idea: 'I can be like that bird,' he thinks . . .

What is Brown's idea? How can he be like a bird? Can he escape from prison?

OXFORD BOOKWORMS LIBRARY

Thriller & Adventure

Escape

Starter (250 headwords)

PHILLIP BURROWS AND MARK FOSTER

Escape

OXFORD UNIVERSITY PRESS

OXFORD
UNIVERSITY PRESS

Great Clarendon Street, Oxford OX2 6DP

Oxford University Press is a department of the University of Oxford.
It furthers the University's objective of excellence in research, scholarship,
and education by publishing worldwide in

Oxford New York

Auckland Cape Town Dar es Salaam Hong Kong Karachi
Kuala Lumpur Madrid Melbourne Mexico City Nairobi
New Delhi Shanghai Taipei Toronto

With offices in

Argentina Austria Brazil Chile Czech Republic France Greece
Guatemala Hungary Italy Japan Poland Portugal Singapore
South Korea Switzerland Thailand Turkey Ukraine Vietnam

CONTENTS

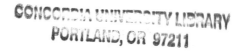

ESCAPE

I'm innocent! Why don't they believe me?

Five years! I must stay in this prison for five years! All I do is read. This is no life. I must get out of here.

You're a thief. Everybody hates thieves.

I'm not a thief. I'm an innocent man.

You're not innocent. Why are you in prison? Can you answer that? Now, eat and be quiet.

I'm not hungry!

CRASH!

Wait a minute. I've got an idea. I can be like that bird.

There's a photograph. It's in one of these books, and it shows the country near the prison. Where is it?

Yes! it's here. Here's the prison. And over here . . .

OK. Tomorrow I'm leaving.

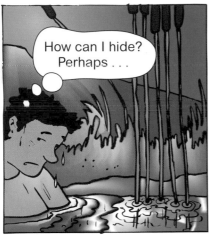

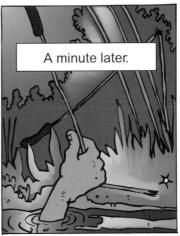

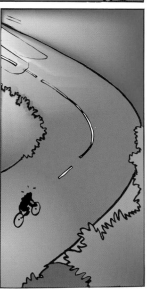

There is a noise. Brown opens his eyes.

What's that?

Come on then, Daisy. On your feet, Clover.

MOO!

MOO!

Good, I'm safe. The farmer's going away.

These are prison clothes. I need some different clothes.

Brown looks out of his window for a long time.

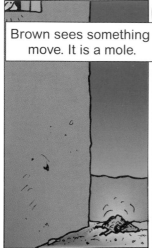

Brown sees something move. It is a mole.

Wait a minute!

That mole's making a tunnel.

Dig...
dig...

I've got an idea.

GLOSSARY

believe think someone is telling the truth

electric an electric fence works by using electricity

escape run away from prison

free (*adj*) not in prison

hate strongly dislike

hide go to a place where no one can see you

hurt a broken leg hurts

idea a clever thought

innocent (*adj*) doing no wrong

lie you lie on your back when you sleep

ouch a noise you make when you hurt yourself

safe you are safe when no one can hurt you

shush a noise you say to make someone quiet

snore a noise some people make when they sleep

stomach the part of your body where food goes

thief someone who takes something that is not theirs

turn change the way you are going

way a direction or path

Escape

ACTIVITIES

ACTIVITIES

Before Reading

1 **Look at the front and back cover of the book and answer these questions.**

1 Who is Brown?

  a ☐ A cross country runner.

  b ☐ A prisoner.

  c ☐ A farmer.

2 What do you think happens to Brown?

  a ☐ Someone catches Brown.

  b ☐ Brown escapes.

  c ☐ Someone shoots Brown.

3 Do you think Brown is

  a ☐ . . . a thief?

  b ☐ . . . a murderer?

  c ☐ . . . an innocent man?

2 **Read the story introduction on the first page of the book and answer these questions.**

1 Do the prison guards like Brown?

2 Brown has an idea. What is it, do you think?

ACTIVITIES

While Reading

1 **Match the words with the pictures.**

a ☐ 'Good, I'm safe. The farmer's going away.'

b ☐ 'Be careful, Brown. Don't fall now.'

c ☐ 'Ow!'

d ☐ 'I'm not hungry.'

2 Read pages 1–12.
Are the following true (T) or false (F)?

	T	F
1 Brown must stay in prison for ten years.	☐	☐
2 Someone sees Brown escape.	☐	☐
3 The guard brings Brown his dinner.	☐	☐
4 Brown sees a dog out of the window.	☐	☐
5 The guard hides from Brown.	☐	☐
6 Brown hides in a ditch.	☐	☐

3 Read pages 13–24 and answer the following questions.

Who

1 . . . hides in the river?

2 . . . is sitting by the side of the road?

3 . . . says: 'He does snore!'?

4 . . . wants her clothes back?

5 . . . wants three big pizzas?

6 . . . says: 'Nobody escapes from me'?

7 . . . is digging a tunnel?

Why

8 . . . does Brown stop cycling?

9 . . . does Brown change his clothes?

10 . . . can't Brown climb the fence?

11 . . . is Brown's box not on the plane?

What

12 . . . does Brown take from the camper?

13 . . . does Brown say to the chickens?

14 . . . does the woman pilot want to eat?

15 . . . does Brown do when he is back in his cell?

ACTIVITIES

After Reading

1 Use these words to join the sentences together.

but   and   when   so
1 Brown is in prison. He says he is innocent.
2 Brown jumps in the ditch. The guards shine the light.
3 The dogs chase Brown. He hides in the water.
4 One pilot wants one pizza. The other pilot wants five.
5 Brown cannot escape by plane. He has another idea.

2 Write a short letter to a friend. Tell them what the story is about. Include these words in your letter:

escape   prison   guard   farmer   plane   box   light
fence   catch   fly   dogs   book

....
....
....
....
....
....
....
....
....
....

3 Write a different ending by filling in the speech bubbles.

ABOUT THE AUTHORS

Mark Foster and Phillip Burrows have worked as a writer/ illustrator team since 1991. They were born three years and many miles apart, but they are very nearly twins. They drive the same car, work on the same computers, and wear the same wellington boots – but not at the same time! They spend all the money they get from writing on gadgets, but please don't tell their wives. Mark and Phill have worked together on several Bookworms titles, including the two thriller and adventure stories *Taxi of Terror* (Starter) and *Orca* (Starter). When they meet to write, they like to go to expensive hotels, eat chips dipped in coffee, and laugh at their own jokes.

OXFORD BOOKWORMS LIBRARY

Classics • Crime & Mystery • Factfiles • Fantasy & Horror
Human Interest • Playscripts • Thriller & Adventure
True Stories • World Stories

The OXFORD BOOKWORMS LIBRARY provides enjoyable reading in English, with a wide range of classic and modern fiction, non-fiction, and plays. It includes original and adapted texts in seven carefully graded language stages, which take learners from beginner to advanced level. An overview is given on the next pages.

All Stage 1 titles are available as audio recordings, as well as over eighty other titles from Starter to Stage 6. All Starters and many titles at Stages 1 to 4 are specially recommended for younger learners. Every Bookworm is illustrated, and Starters and Factfiles have full-colour illustrations.

The OXFORD BOOKWORMS LIBRARY also offers extensive support. Each book contains an introduction to the story, notes about the author, a glossary, and activities. Additional resources include tests and worksheets, and answers for these and for the activities in the books. There is advice on running a class library, using audio recordings, and the many ways of using Oxford Bookworms in reading programmes. Resource materials are available on the website <www.oup.com/bookworms>.

The *Oxford Bookworms Collection* is a series for advanced learners. It consists of volumes of short stories by well-known authors, both classic and modern. Texts are not abridged or adapted in any way, but carefully selected to be accessible to the advanced student.

You can find details and a full list of titles in the *Oxford Bookworms Library Catalogue* and *Oxford English Language Teaching Catalogues*, and on the website <www.oup.com/bookworms>.

THE OXFORD BOOKWORMS LIBRARY
GRADING AND SAMPLE EXTRACTS

STARTER • 250 HEADWORDS

present simple – present continuous – imperative –
can/cannot, must – *going to* (future) – simple gerunds …

Her phone is ringing – but where is it?

Sally gets out of bed and looks in her bag. No phone. She looks under the bed. No phone. Then she looks behind the door. There is her phone. Sally picks up her phone and answers it. *Sally's Phone*

STAGE 1 • 400 HEADWORDS

… past simple – coordination with *and*, *but*, *or* –
subordination with *before*, *after*, *when*, *because*, *so* …

I knew him in Persia. He was a famous builder and I worked with him there. For a time I was his friend, but not for long. When he came to Paris, I came after him – I wanted to watch him. He was a very clever, very dangerous man. *The Phantom of the Opera*

STAGE 2 • 700 HEADWORDS

… present perfect – *will* (future) – *(don't) have to, must not, could* –
comparison of adjectives – simple *if* clauses – past continuous –
tag questions – *ask/tell* + infinitive …

While I was writing these words in my diary, I decided what to do. I must try to escape. I shall try to get down the wall outside. The window is high above the ground, but I have to try. I shall take some of the gold with me – if I escape, perhaps it will be helpful later. *Dracula*

STAGE 3 • 1000 HEADWORDS

... should, may – present perfect continuous – *used to* – past perfect –
causative – relative clauses – indirect statements ...

Of course, it was most important that no one should see
Colin, Mary, or Dickon entering the secret garden. So Colin
gave orders to the gardeners that they must all keep away
from that part of the garden in future. *The Secret Garden*

STAGE 4 • 1400 HEADWORDS

... past perfect continuous – passive (simple forms) –
would conditional clauses – indirect questions –
relatives with *where/when* – gerunds after prepositions/phrases ...

I was glad. Now Hyde could not show his face to the world
again. If he did, every honest man in London would be
proud to report him to the police. *Dr Jekyll and Mr Hyde*

STAGE 5 • 1800 HEADWORDS

... future continuous – future perfect –
passive (modals, continuous forms) –
would have conditional clauses – modals + perfect infinitive ...

If he had spoken Estella's name, I would have hit him. I was so
angry with him, and so depressed about my future, that I could
not eat the breakfast. Instead I went straight to the old house.
Great Expectations

STAGE 6 • 2500 HEADWORDS

... passive (infinitives, gerunds) – advanced modal meanings –
clauses of concession, condition

When I stepped up to the piano, I was confident. It was as if I
knew that the prodigy side of me really did exist. And when I
started to play, I was so caught up in how lovely I looked that
I didn't worry how I would sound. *The Joy Luck Club*

BOOKWORMS · THRILLER & ADVENTURE · STARTER

Drive into Danger

ROSEMARY BORDER

'I can drive a truck,' says Kim on her first day at work in the office. When Kim's passenger Andy finds something strange under the truck things get dangerous – very dangerous.

BOOKWORMS · THRILLER & ADVENTURE · STARTER

Taxi of Terror

PHILLIP BURROWS AND MARK FOSTER

'How does it work?' Jack asks when he opens his present – a mobile phone. Later that night, Jack is a prisoner in a taxi in the empty streets of the dark city. He now tries his mobile phone for the first time. Can it save his life?

BOOKWORMS · CRIME & MYSTERY · STARTER

Oranges in the Snow

PHILLIP BURROWS AND MARK FOSTER

'Everything's ready now. We can do the experiment,' says your
assistant Joe.

You are the famous scientist Mary Durie working in a laboratory
in Alaska. When you discover something very new and valuable,
other people want to try to steal your idea – can you stop them
before they escape?

BOOKWORMS · FANTASY & HORROR · STARTER

Starman

PHILLIP BURROWS AND MARK FOSTER

The empty centre of Australia. The sun is hot and there are not
many people. And when Bill meets a man, alone, standing on an
empty road a long way from anywhere, he is surprised and worried.

And Bill is right to be worried. Because there is something
strange about the man he meets. Very strange . . .

BOOKWORMS · THRILLER & ADVENTURE · STAGE 1

Goodbye, Mr Hollywood

JOHN ESCOTT

Nick Lortz is sitting outside a café in Whistler, a village in the Canadian mountains, when a stranger comes and sits next to him. She's young, pretty, and has a beautiful smile. Nick is happy to sit and talk with her.

But why does she call Nick 'Mr Hollywood'? Why does she give him a big kiss when she leaves? And who is the man at the next table – the man with short white hair?

Nick learns the answers to these questions three long days later – in a police station on Vancouver Island.

BOOKWORMS · THRILLER & ADVENTURE · STAGE 1

White Death

TIM VICARY

Sarah Harland is nineteen, and she is in prison. At the airport, they find heroin in her bag. So, now she is waiting to go to court. If the court decides that it was her heroin, then she must die.

She says she did not do it. But if she did not, who did? Only two people can help Sarah: her mother, and an old boyfriend who does not love her now. Can they work together? Can they find the real criminal before it is too late?